50 Cast Iron Skillet Recipes for Home

By: Kelly Johnson

Table of Contents

- Classic Cast Iron Skillet Cornbread
- Pan-Seared Ribeye Steak
- Skillet Chicken Pot Pie
- Cast Iron Skillet Pizza
- Dutch Baby Pancake
- Cast Iron Skillet Apple Crisp
- Southern Style Fried Chicken
- Skillet Mac and Cheese
- Sizzling Fajitas
- Cornbread-Stuffed Pork Chops
- Skillet Garlic Butter Shrimp
- Cast Iron Skillet Lasagna
- Cast Iron Skillet Cornbread Stuffing
- Spanish Tortilla
- Cajun Blackened Fish
- Skillet Chicken Alfredo
- Cast Iron Skillet Breakfast Hash
- Skillet Sausage and Peppers
- Crispy Cast Iron Skillet Chicken Thighs
- Cast Iron Skillet Cobbler
- Pan-Seared Scallops
- Skillet Cornbread with Honey Butter
- Cast Iron Skillet Tacos
- Spinach and Feta Frittata
- Skillet Pork Tenderloin with Mustard Sauce
- Cast Iron Skillet Cinnamon Rolls
- Skillet Shepherd's Pie
- One-Pot Jambalaya
- Lemon Herb Roast Chicken
- Cast Iron Skillet Biscuits and Gravy
- Skillet Beef Stir-Fry
- Cast Iron Skillet Gooey Butter Cake
- Skillet Chicken Enchiladas
- Cast Iron Skillet Caramelized Onion Dip
- Skillet Ratatouille

- Cast Iron Skillet Blueberry Pancakes
- Shrimp and Grits
- Skillet Beef and Broccoli
- Cast Iron Skillet Chocolate Chip Cookie
- Skillet Corned Beef Hash
- Cast Iron Skillet BBQ Ribs
- Skillet Lemon Garlic Butter Salmon
- Cast Iron Skillet French Toast
- Skillet Vegetable Paella
- Cast Iron Skillet Peach Pie
- Skillet Chicken Marsala
- Cast Iron Skillet S'mores Dip
- Skillet Sweet Potato Hash
- Cast Iron Skillet Lemon Bars
- Skillet Cajun Shrimp Pasta

Classic Cast Iron Skillet Cornbread

Ingredients:

- 1 cup yellow cornmeal
- 1 cup all-purpose flour
- 1/4 cup granulated sugar
- 1 tablespoon baking powder
- 1 teaspoon salt
- 1 cup buttermilk
- 2 large eggs
- 1/2 cup unsalted butter, melted
- Optional: 1/2 cup corn kernels (fresh, canned, or frozen)

Instructions:

1. Preheat your oven to 400°F (200°C). Place a 10-inch cast iron skillet in the oven while it preheats.
2. In a large mixing bowl, whisk together the cornmeal, flour, sugar, baking powder, and salt until well combined.
3. In a separate bowl, whisk together the buttermilk and eggs until smooth.
4. Pour the wet ingredients into the dry ingredients and mix until just combined. Be careful not to overmix; a few lumps are okay.
5. Carefully remove the hot skillet from the oven using oven mitts. Add the melted butter to the skillet, swirling to coat the bottom and sides evenly.
6. Pour the batter into the hot skillet, spreading it evenly with a spatula. If using corn kernels, sprinkle them evenly over the top of the batter.
7. Place the skillet back in the oven and bake for 20-25 minutes, or until the cornbread is golden brown on top and a toothpick inserted into the center comes out clean.
8. Once baked, remove the skillet from the oven and let the cornbread cool for a few minutes before slicing and serving.
9. Enjoy your classic cast iron skillet cornbread warm with butter, honey, or your favorite chili or soup.

Note: Be cautious when handling the hot cast iron skillet, as it retains heat very well. Use oven mitts or a thick towel to protect your hands.

Pan-Seared Ribeye Steak

Ingredients:

- 2 ribeye steaks, about 1 inch thick
- Salt and freshly ground black pepper, to taste
- 2 tablespoons vegetable oil or clarified butter
- Optional: Garlic cloves, fresh thyme, or rosemary for extra flavor

Instructions:

1. Remove the ribeye steaks from the refrigerator and let them sit at room temperature for about 30 minutes to ensure even cooking.
2. Pat the steaks dry with paper towels to remove excess moisture. Season both sides generously with salt and freshly ground black pepper.
3. Heat a large cast iron skillet over medium-high heat. Add the vegetable oil or clarified butter to the skillet and heat until shimmering.
4. Carefully place the seasoned ribeye steaks in the hot skillet. If desired, add whole garlic cloves, fresh thyme, or rosemary to the skillet for extra flavor.
5. Cook the steaks undisturbed for about 4-5 minutes on one side, or until a deep brown crust forms.
6. Flip the steaks using tongs and cook for an additional 4-5 minutes on the other side for medium-rare doneness. Adjust the cooking time according to your preference for doneness (see notes below).
7. Once cooked to your liking, transfer the steaks to a cutting board or plate and let them rest for 5-10 minutes to allow the juices to redistribute.
8. Slice the ribeye steaks against the grain and serve immediately with your favorite side dishes.

Notes:

- For medium-rare doneness, aim for an internal temperature of around 130-135°F (54-57°C) when using an instant-read thermometer.
- Cooking times may vary depending on the thickness of the steaks and the heat of your skillet. Adjust accordingly for thicker or thinner cuts.
- Avoid overcrowding the skillet to ensure proper searing and browning of the steaks.
- Feel free to customize the seasoning with your favorite herbs and spices for added flavor.

Skillet Chicken Pot Pie

Ingredients:

- 2 tablespoons unsalted butter
- 1 onion, finely chopped
- 2 carrots, diced
- 2 celery stalks, diced
- 2 cloves garlic, minced
- 1/4 cup all-purpose flour
- 2 cups chicken broth
- 1 cup milk (whole or 2%)
- 2 cups cooked chicken, diced or shredded
- 1 cup frozen peas
- Salt and pepper, to taste
- 1 tablespoon fresh thyme leaves (or 1 teaspoon dried thyme)
- 1 sheet of puff pastry, thawed if frozen
- 1 egg, beaten (for egg wash)

Instructions:

1. Preheat your oven to 400°F (200°C).
2. In a large oven-safe skillet, melt the butter over medium heat. Add the chopped onion, carrots, and celery. Cook, stirring occasionally, until the vegetables are softened, about 5-7 minutes.
3. Add the minced garlic to the skillet and cook for an additional minute until fragrant.
4. Sprinkle the flour over the vegetables and stir to combine, cooking for 1-2 minutes to remove the raw flour taste.
5. Slowly pour in the chicken broth and milk, stirring constantly to prevent lumps from forming. Bring the mixture to a simmer and cook until thickened, about 5 minutes.
6. Stir in the cooked chicken, frozen peas, thyme leaves, salt, and pepper. Taste and adjust seasoning if needed.
7. Roll out the puff pastry sheet on a lightly floured surface to fit the size of your skillet. Place the pastry over the filling in the skillet, tucking any excess pastry around the edges.
8. Brush the beaten egg over the top of the pastry for a golden finish.
9. Cut a few slits in the pastry to allow steam to escape during baking.
10. Place the skillet in the preheated oven and bake for 25-30 minutes, or until the pastry is golden brown and the filling is bubbly.
11. Once baked, remove the skillet from the oven and let it cool for a few minutes before serving.
12. Serve the skillet chicken pot pie warm and enjoy!

Note: You can customize this recipe by adding other vegetables like mushrooms or potatoes, or by using leftover turkey instead of chicken. Adjust the seasoning according to your taste preferences.

Cast Iron Skillet Pizza

Ingredients:

- 1 lb pizza dough, store-bought or homemade
- 1/2 cup pizza sauce
- 1 1/2 cups shredded mozzarella cheese
- Toppings of your choice (pepperoni, bell peppers, onions, mushrooms, etc.)
- Olive oil, for brushing
- Cornmeal or flour, for dusting

Instructions:

1. Preheat your oven to 500°F (260°C) with a rack positioned in the middle.
2. Lightly oil a 10 or 12-inch cast iron skillet, ensuring the bottom and sides are coated evenly.
3. On a lightly floured surface, roll out the pizza dough into a circle slightly larger than the skillet.
4. Carefully transfer the rolled-out dough to the prepared skillet, gently pressing it into the bottom and up the sides of the skillet.
5. Spread the pizza sauce evenly over the dough, leaving a small border around the edges.
6. Sprinkle the shredded mozzarella cheese over the sauce, covering the entire surface.
7. Add your desired toppings evenly over the cheese layer.
8. Place the skillet on the stovetop over medium heat and cook for 3-5 minutes, or until the bottom of the crust is golden brown and begins to crisp up.
9. Once the bottom is cooked, transfer the skillet to the preheated oven and bake for an additional 10-12 minutes, or until the cheese is bubbly and the crust is golden brown.
10. Carefully remove the skillet from the oven using oven mitts.
11. Let the pizza cool in the skillet for a few minutes before using a spatula to transfer it to a cutting board.
12. Slice the pizza into wedges and serve hot. Enjoy your delicious cast iron skillet pizza!

Dutch Baby Pancake

Ingredients:

- 3 large eggs
- 2/3 cup all-purpose flour
- 2/3 cup milk
- 1 tablespoon granulated sugar
- 1/2 teaspoon vanilla extract
- Pinch of salt
- 3 tablespoons unsalted butter
- Powdered sugar, for dusting
- Fresh fruit, such as berries, for serving (optional)
- Maple syrup, for serving (optional)

Instructions:

1. Preheat your oven to 425°F (220°C).
2. In a blender, combine the eggs, flour, milk, sugar, vanilla extract, and salt. Blend until the batter is smooth and well combined, with no lumps remaining.
3. Place the butter in a 10-inch cast iron skillet and put it in the preheated oven until the butter melts and starts to sizzle, about 3-5 minutes.
4. Carefully remove the skillet from the oven and swirl the melted butter to coat the bottom and sides evenly.
5. Pour the batter into the hot skillet over the melted butter.
6. Return the skillet to the oven and bake for 15-20 minutes, or until the pancake is puffed up and golden brown around the edges.
7. Remove the Dutch baby pancake from the oven and sprinkle with powdered sugar.
8. Serve immediately, either plain or topped with fresh fruit and a drizzle of maple syrup if desired.
9. Enjoy your delicious Dutch baby pancake straight from the oven!

Cast Iron Skillet Apple Crisp

Ingredients:

- 4-5 medium-sized apples, peeled, cored, and sliced (such as Granny Smith, Honeycrisp, or Fuji)
- 1 tablespoon lemon juice
- 1/4 cup granulated sugar
- 1 teaspoon ground cinnamon
- 1/4 teaspoon ground nutmeg
- 1/2 cup all-purpose flour
- 1/2 cup old-fashioned rolled oats
- 1/4 cup packed brown sugar
- 1/4 teaspoon salt
- 1/2 cup unsalted butter, cold and diced
- Vanilla ice cream or whipped cream, for serving (optional)

Instructions:

1. Preheat your oven to 375°F (190°C).
2. In a large bowl, toss the sliced apples with lemon juice to prevent browning.
3. Add the granulated sugar, ground cinnamon, and ground nutmeg to the apples. Toss until the apples are evenly coated with the sugar and spices.
4. Transfer the seasoned apples to a 10-inch cast iron skillet, spreading them out evenly.
5. In a separate bowl, combine the all-purpose flour, rolled oats, brown sugar, and salt.
6. Add the diced cold butter to the flour mixture. Using a pastry cutter or your fingers, work the butter into the dry ingredients until the mixture resembles coarse crumbs.
7. Sprinkle the crumb topping evenly over the apples in the skillet.
8. Place the skillet in the preheated oven and bake for 30-35 minutes, or until the topping is golden brown and the apples are tender and bubbling.
9. Remove the skillet from the oven and let the apple crisp cool for a few minutes before serving.
10. Serve warm with a scoop of vanilla ice cream or a dollop of whipped cream, if desired.
11. Enjoy your delicious cast iron skillet apple crisp!

Southern Style Fried Chicken

Ingredients:

- 8 pieces of chicken (drumsticks, thighs, breasts, or a combination)
- 2 cups buttermilk
- 2 cups all-purpose flour
- 1 tablespoon salt
- 1 tablespoon black pepper
- 1 tablespoon paprika
- 1 teaspoon garlic powder
- 1 teaspoon onion powder
- 1/2 teaspoon cayenne pepper (optional, for heat)
- Vegetable oil, for frying

Instructions:

1. Place the chicken pieces in a large bowl or resealable plastic bag. Pour the buttermilk over the chicken, ensuring it is completely coated. Cover the bowl or seal the bag and refrigerate for at least 4 hours or overnight.
2. In a shallow dish, combine the all-purpose flour, salt, black pepper, paprika, garlic powder, onion powder, and cayenne pepper (if using). Mix well to combine.
3. Remove the marinated chicken from the refrigerator and let it come to room temperature for about 30 minutes.
4. Heat vegetable oil in a large cast iron skillet or Dutch oven to 350°F (175°C).
5. Remove each piece of chicken from the buttermilk, allowing any excess to drip off, then dredge it in the seasoned flour mixture, coating it thoroughly. Shake off any excess flour.
6. Carefully place the coated chicken pieces in the hot oil, making sure not to overcrowd the skillet. Fry in batches if necessary.
7. Fry the chicken for about 15-20 minutes, turning occasionally, until golden brown and cooked through. The internal temperature of the chicken should reach 165°F (74°C).
8. Once cooked, transfer the fried chicken to a wire rack set over a baking sheet or paper towels to drain any excess oil.
9. Allow the chicken to rest for a few minutes before serving to let the juices redistribute.
10. Serve the Southern style fried chicken hot, with your favorite sides such as mashed potatoes, coleslaw, or biscuits.
11. Enjoy your deliciously crispy and flavorful Southern fried chicken!

Skillet Mac and Cheese

Ingredients:

- 8 ounces (about 2 cups) elbow macaroni or pasta of your choice
- 2 tablespoons unsalted butter
- 2 tablespoons all-purpose flour
- 2 cups whole milk
- 2 cups shredded sharp cheddar cheese
- 1 cup shredded mozzarella cheese
- 1/2 cup grated Parmesan cheese
- 1 teaspoon Dijon mustard (optional)
- Salt and black pepper, to taste
- Optional toppings: crispy bacon bits, chopped green onions, breadcrumbs

Instructions:

1. Cook the macaroni according to the package instructions in a large pot of salted boiling water until al dente. Drain and set aside.
2. In the same pot or a large skillet, melt the butter over medium heat.
3. Stir in the flour and cook for 1-2 minutes, stirring constantly, to make a roux.
4. Gradually whisk in the milk, stirring constantly to avoid lumps.
5. Cook the sauce for 3-4 minutes, or until it thickens and coats the back of a spoon.
6. Reduce the heat to low and gradually stir in the shredded cheddar cheese, mozzarella cheese, and Parmesan cheese until melted and smooth.
7. Stir in the Dijon mustard, if using, and season the cheese sauce with salt and black pepper to taste.
8. Add the cooked macaroni to the cheese sauce, stirring until well combined and evenly coated.
9. If desired, sprinkle the top of the mac and cheese with crispy bacon bits, chopped green onions, or breadcrumbs for extra flavor and texture.
10. Serve the skillet mac and cheese hot, straight from the skillet.
11. Enjoy your creamy and cheesy skillet mac and cheese!

Sizzling Fajitas

Ingredients: For the Marinade:

- 1/4 cup olive oil
- 3 tablespoons lime juice
- 3 cloves garlic, minced
- 1 teaspoon ground cumin
- 1 teaspoon chili powder
- 1/2 teaspoon smoked paprika
- 1/2 teaspoon dried oregano
- 1/4 teaspoon cayenne pepper (optional)
- Salt and black pepper, to taste

For the Fajitas:

- 1 lb (450g) steak (flank steak, skirt steak, or chicken breast), thinly sliced against the grain
- 1 large onion, thinly sliced
- 1 large bell pepper (any color), thinly sliced
- 8-10 small flour tortillas, warmed
- Optional toppings: salsa, guacamole, sour cream, shredded cheese, chopped cilantro, lime wedges

Instructions:

1. In a large bowl, whisk together the olive oil, lime juice, minced garlic, ground cumin, chili powder, smoked paprika, dried oregano, cayenne pepper (if using), salt, and black pepper to make the marinade.
2. Add the thinly sliced steak or chicken to the marinade, ensuring it's well coated. Cover and refrigerate for at least 30 minutes, or up to 4 hours, to marinate.
3. Heat a large cast iron skillet or grill pan over medium-high heat. Once hot, add the marinated steak or chicken along with any excess marinade to the skillet.
4. Cook the meat for 3-4 minutes per side, or until browned and cooked through. Remove the cooked meat from the skillet and set aside on a plate.
5. In the same skillet, add the thinly sliced onion and bell pepper. Cook for 5-6 minutes, or until softened and slightly charred, stirring occasionally.
6. Return the cooked meat to the skillet with the onions and peppers. Toss everything together to combine and heat through for another minute.
7. Remove the skillet from the heat and serve the sizzling fajitas immediately with warmed flour tortillas and your choice of toppings.
8. Allow everyone to assemble their own fajitas at the table, filling the tortillas with the meat and vegetable mixture and adding toppings as desired.
9. Enjoy your sizzling fajitas straight from the skillet with all the delicious toppings!

Cornbread-Stuffed Pork Chops

Ingredients: For the Cornbread:

- 1 cup yellow cornmeal
- 1 cup all-purpose flour
- 1 tablespoon baking powder
- 1/2 teaspoon baking soda
- 1 teaspoon salt
- 1/4 cup granulated sugar
- 1 cup buttermilk
- 2 large eggs
- 1/4 cup unsalted butter, melted
- 1/2 cup corn kernels (fresh, canned, or frozen)
- 2 tablespoons chopped fresh parsley (optional)

For the Pork Chops:

- 4 thick-cut boneless pork chops
- Salt and black pepper, to taste
- 1 tablespoon olive oil
- 1 small onion, finely chopped
- 2 cloves garlic, minced
- 1/2 cup diced bell pepper (any color)
- 1/2 cup diced celery
- 1 teaspoon dried thyme
- 1 teaspoon dried sage
- 1/2 cup chicken or vegetable broth
- 1 tablespoon unsalted butter

Instructions:

1. Preheat your oven to 375°F (190°C). Grease a 9x9-inch baking dish or line it with parchment paper.
2. In a large mixing bowl, whisk together the cornmeal, flour, baking powder, baking soda, salt, and granulated sugar until well combined.
3. In another bowl, whisk together the buttermilk, eggs, and melted butter until smooth.
4. Pour the wet ingredients into the dry ingredients and stir until just combined. Be careful not to overmix. Fold in the corn kernels and chopped parsley, if using.
5. Pour the cornbread batter into the prepared baking dish and spread it out evenly. Bake for 20-25 minutes, or until a toothpick inserted into the center comes out clean. Remove from the oven and let it cool slightly.
6. While the cornbread is baking, prepare the pork chops. Using a sharp knife, make a horizontal slit along the side of each pork chop to create a pocket for stuffing. Be careful not to cut all the way through.

7. Season the pork chops generously with salt and black pepper, both inside and out.
8. In a skillet over medium heat, heat the olive oil. Add the chopped onion, garlic, bell pepper, and celery. Cook until the vegetables are softened, about 5 minutes.
9. Stir in the dried thyme and sage, then remove the skillet from the heat.
10. Crumble the baked cornbread into the skillet with the cooked vegetables and mix well to combine. If the mixture seems too dry, add a splash of chicken or vegetable broth to moisten it.
11. Stuff each pork chop with the cornbread mixture, pressing gently to pack it in. Secure the opening with toothpicks, if necessary.
12. In the same skillet used for the vegetables, melt the butter over medium-high heat. Add the stuffed pork chops and sear on both sides until golden brown, about 3-4 minutes per side.
13. Pour the chicken or vegetable broth into the skillet around the pork chops. Transfer the skillet to the preheated oven and bake for 20-25 minutes, or until the pork chops are cooked through and reach an internal temperature of 145°F (63°C).
14. Remove the skillet from the oven and let the pork chops rest for a few minutes before serving. Serve the cornbread-stuffed pork chops hot, garnished with chopped parsley if desired. Enjoy!

Skillet Garlic Butter Shrimp

Ingredients:

- 1 lb (450g) large shrimp, peeled and deveined
- Salt and black pepper, to taste
- 3 tablespoons unsalted butter
- 4 cloves garlic, minced
- 1 tablespoon fresh lemon juice
- 2 tablespoons chopped fresh parsley, for garnish
- Lemon wedges, for serving
- Cooked pasta, rice, or crusty bread, for serving (optional)

Instructions:

1. Pat the shrimp dry with paper towels and season with salt and black pepper to taste.
2. In a large skillet, melt the butter over medium heat.
3. Add the minced garlic to the skillet and cook for 1-2 minutes, stirring frequently, until fragrant.
4. Add the seasoned shrimp to the skillet in a single layer. Cook for 2-3 minutes, or until the shrimp start to turn pink on one side.
5. Flip the shrimp and continue cooking for another 2-3 minutes, or until they are cooked through and opaque.
6. Stir in the fresh lemon juice and chopped parsley, tossing the shrimp to coat evenly.
7. Remove the skillet from the heat.
8. Serve the skillet garlic butter shrimp hot, garnished with additional chopped parsley and lemon wedges on the side.
9. Enjoy your flavorful and buttery skillet garlic butter shrimp as is or serve them over cooked pasta, rice, or with crusty bread to soak up the delicious sauce.

Cast Iron Skillet Lasagna

Ingredients:

- 1 lb (450g) ground beef or Italian sausage
- 1 onion, finely chopped
- 3 cloves garlic, minced
- 1 can (14 oz) crushed tomatoes
- 1 can (6 oz) tomato paste
- 1 teaspoon dried basil
- 1 teaspoon dried oregano
- Salt and black pepper, to taste
- 8 lasagna noodles, uncooked
- 2 cups ricotta cheese
- 1 large egg
- 2 cups shredded mozzarella cheese
- 1/2 cup grated Parmesan cheese
- Fresh basil leaves, for garnish (optional)

Instructions:

1. Preheat your oven to 375°F (190°C).
2. In a large cast iron skillet, cook the ground beef or Italian sausage over medium heat until browned and cooked through, breaking it up with a spoon as it cooks.
3. Add the chopped onion and minced garlic to the skillet with the cooked meat. Cook for 2-3 minutes, or until the onion is softened and translucent.
4. Stir in the crushed tomatoes, tomato paste, dried basil, dried oregano, salt, and black pepper. Simmer the sauce for 5-10 minutes, stirring occasionally, to allow the flavors to meld.
5. While the sauce is simmering, break the lasagna noodles into smaller pieces that will fit into the skillet.
6. In a medium bowl, combine the ricotta cheese and egg until well mixed.
7. Once the sauce is ready, remove the skillet from the heat. Arrange half of the broken lasagna noodles over the sauce in an even layer.
8. Spread half of the ricotta mixture over the noodles, followed by half of the shredded mozzarella cheese and half of the grated Parmesan cheese.
9. Repeat the layers with the remaining noodles, ricotta mixture, mozzarella cheese, and Parmesan cheese.
10. Cover the skillet with aluminum foil and bake in the preheated oven for 25-30 minutes.
11. Remove the foil and bake for an additional 10-15 minutes, or until the cheese is melted and bubbly and the lasagna noodles are tender.
12. Once baked, remove the skillet from the oven and let the lasagna cool for a few minutes before slicing.
13. Garnish with fresh basil leaves, if desired, before serving.
14. Serve the skillet lasagna hot and enjoy your delicious, cheesy creation!

Cast Iron Skillet Cornbread Stuffing

Ingredients:

- 1 batch of cornbread (you can use your favorite recipe or a store-bought mix)
- 2 tablespoons unsalted butter
- 1 onion, finely chopped
- 2 celery stalks, finely chopped
- 2 cloves garlic, minced
- 1 teaspoon dried sage
- 1 teaspoon dried thyme
- Salt and pepper to taste
- 1/2 cup chicken or vegetable broth
- 2 eggs, beaten
- 1/4 cup chopped fresh parsley
- Optional: 1/2 cup chopped pecans or walnuts

Instructions:

1. Preheat your oven to 350°F (175°C).
2. Crumble the cornbread into a large mixing bowl and set aside.
3. In a cast iron skillet, melt the butter over medium heat.
4. Add the chopped onion and celery to the skillet. Sauté until they begin to soften, about 5-7 minutes.
5. Add the minced garlic, sage, thyme, salt, and pepper to the skillet. Cook for an additional 1-2 minutes until fragrant.
6. Pour the vegetable mixture over the crumbled cornbread in the mixing bowl. Mix well to combine.
7. In a separate bowl, whisk together the chicken or vegetable broth and beaten eggs.
8. Gradually pour the broth and egg mixture over the cornbread mixture, stirring until evenly combined. Adjust the amount of liquid as needed to achieve your desired consistency.
9. Stir in the chopped parsley and nuts (if using).
10. Transfer the mixture back into the cast iron skillet, spreading it out evenly.
11. Bake in the preheated oven for 25-30 minutes, or until the top is golden brown and crispy.
12. Serve hot and enjoy your delicious cast iron skillet cornbread stuffing!

This stuffing is a perfect side dish for any holiday meal or gathering. Feel free to customize it with your favorite herbs, spices, and add-ins to suit your taste preferences.

Spanish Tortilla

Ingredients:

- 4-5 medium potatoes, peeled and thinly sliced
- 1 onion, thinly sliced
- 6 large eggs
- Salt and pepper to taste
- Olive oil for frying

Instructions:

1. Heat about 1/2 inch of olive oil in a large skillet over medium heat. Once the oil is hot, add the sliced potatoes and onions. Cook, stirring occasionally, until the potatoes are tender but not browned, about 10-15 minutes. Remove from heat and drain excess oil.
2. In a large mixing bowl, beat the eggs together with salt and pepper.
3. Add the cooked potatoes and onions to the egg mixture. Stir gently to combine, ensuring that the potatoes and onions are evenly coated with the eggs.
4. Heat a tablespoon of olive oil in a non-stick skillet over medium heat. Pour the potato and egg mixture into the skillet, spreading it out evenly.
5. Cook the tortilla for about 5-7 minutes, or until the edges start to set and the bottom is lightly golden brown.
6. Carefully flip the tortilla using a large plate or lid to cover the skillet. Slide the tortilla back into the skillet to cook the other side. Cook for an additional 5-7 minutes, or until the tortilla is cooked through and golden brown on both sides.
7. Once cooked, transfer the tortilla to a cutting board and allow it to cool slightly before slicing into wedges.
8. Serve the Spanish Tortilla warm or at room temperature, garnished with fresh herbs or served with aioli or your favorite dipping sauce.

Enjoy your homemade Spanish Tortilla as a delicious appetizer, snack, or light meal!

Cajun Blackened Fish

Ingredients:

- 4 fillets of firm white fish (such as tilapia, catfish, or snapper)
- 2 tablespoons paprika
- 1 tablespoon garlic powder
- 1 tablespoon onion powder
- 1 tablespoon thyme
- 1 tablespoon oregano
- 1 teaspoon cayenne pepper (adjust to taste)
- 1 teaspoon black pepper
- 1 teaspoon white pepper
- 1 teaspoon salt
- 1/2 cup unsalted butter, melted
- Lemon wedges, for serving

Instructions:

1. In a small bowl, combine all the spices: paprika, garlic powder, onion powder, thyme, oregano, cayenne pepper, black pepper, white pepper, and salt. Mix well to create the Cajun seasoning.
2. Preheat a cast iron skillet over high heat until very hot, about 5-7 minutes.
3. Meanwhile, pat the fish fillets dry with paper towels. Brush both sides of each fillet with melted butter.
4. Generously coat each fillet with the Cajun seasoning mixture, pressing it onto the fish to adhere.
5. Carefully place the seasoned fish fillets in the hot skillet. Cook for 2-3 minutes on each side, or until the fish is blackened and cooked through. Cooking time may vary depending on the thickness of the fillets.
6. Once the fish is cooked, remove it from the skillet and transfer it to a serving plate.
7. Serve the Cajun blackened fish hot, garnished with lemon wedges for squeezing over the top.
8. Enjoy your flavorful and spicy Cajun Blackened Fish with your favorite sides, such as rice, vegetables, or a fresh salad.

This dish is perfect for seafood lovers who enjoy a bit of heat and bold flavors. Adjust the level of spiciness according to your preference by increasing or decreasing the amount of cayenne pepper in the seasoning mixture.

Skillet Chicken Alfredo

Ingredients:

- 2 boneless, skinless chicken breasts, sliced thinly
- Salt and pepper to taste
- 2 tablespoons olive oil
- 3 cloves garlic, minced
- 1 cup heavy cream
- 1 cup grated Parmesan cheese
- 1 teaspoon Italian seasoning
- 8 ounces fettuccine or your choice of pasta, cooked according to package instructions
- Chopped fresh parsley, for garnish (optional)

Instructions:

1. Season the sliced chicken breasts with salt and pepper on both sides.
2. Heat the olive oil in a large skillet over medium-high heat. Once hot, add the seasoned chicken slices to the skillet in a single layer. Cook for 3-4 minutes on each side, or until golden brown and cooked through. Remove the cooked chicken from the skillet and set aside.
3. In the same skillet, add the minced garlic and sauté for about 1 minute, or until fragrant.
4. Reduce the heat to medium-low and pour the heavy cream into the skillet. Stir in the grated Parmesan cheese and Italian seasoning. Cook, stirring frequently, until the sauce is smooth and heated through, about 3-4 minutes.
5. Add the cooked pasta to the skillet with the Alfredo sauce, tossing until the pasta is well coated.
6. Return the cooked chicken slices to the skillet, arranging them on top of the pasta and sauce.
7. Allow the chicken and pasta to heat through for another 2-3 minutes.
8. Garnish the skillet chicken Alfredo with chopped fresh parsley, if desired, before serving.
9. Serve hot and enjoy your creamy and delicious skillet chicken Alfredo straight from the pan!

This dish is perfect for a cozy dinner at home and can be served with a side of garlic bread and a crisp green salad for a complete meal. Feel free to customize the recipe by adding your favorite vegetables or herbs to the Alfredo sauce.

Cast Iron Skillet Breakfast Hash

Ingredients:

- 4 medium potatoes, diced into small cubes
- 1 onion, diced
- 1 bell pepper, diced
- 2 cloves garlic, minced
- 8 ounces cooked breakfast sausage, diced
- 4 strips of bacon, cooked and crumbled
- 4 large eggs
- Salt and pepper to taste
- Optional toppings: shredded cheese, chopped fresh herbs, hot sauce

Instructions:

1. Preheat your oven to 400°F (200°C).
2. Heat a cast iron skillet over medium heat. Add a drizzle of oil if necessary.
3. Add the diced potatoes to the skillet and cook, stirring occasionally, until they are golden brown and tender, about 10-12 minutes.
4. Once the potatoes are cooked, add the diced onion, bell pepper, and minced garlic to the skillet. Cook until the vegetables are softened, about 5 minutes.
5. Stir in the cooked breakfast sausage and crumbled bacon. Season with salt and pepper to taste.
6. Create four wells in the hash mixture with the back of a spoon. Crack one egg into each well.
7. Transfer the skillet to the preheated oven and bake for 10-12 minutes, or until the egg whites are set but the yolks are still slightly runny.
8. Carefully remove the skillet from the oven. Sprinkle with shredded cheese if desired and let it melt over the top.
9. Garnish with chopped fresh herbs and a drizzle of hot sauce, if desired.
10. Serve the breakfast hash hot directly from the skillet, allowing everyone to scoop out a portion.

Feel free to customize your breakfast hash with your favorite ingredients, such as diced tomatoes, spinach, mushrooms, or cooked ham. It's a versatile dish that's perfect for using up leftovers or whatever ingredients you have on hand. Enjoy!

Skillet Sausage and Peppers

Ingredients:

- 4 Italian sausages (mild or spicy), sliced into rounds
- 2 bell peppers (red, yellow, or green), sliced
- 1 onion, sliced
- 2 cloves garlic, minced
- 1 can (14.5 ounces) diced tomatoes
- 1 teaspoon dried oregano
- 1 teaspoon dried basil
- Salt and pepper to taste
- Olive oil for cooking
- Fresh parsley, chopped, for garnish (optional)

Instructions:

1. Heat a drizzle of olive oil in a large skillet over medium-high heat.
2. Add the sliced Italian sausages to the skillet and cook until browned on both sides, about 5-7 minutes. Remove the sausages from the skillet and set aside.
3. In the same skillet, add a bit more olive oil if needed. Add the sliced bell peppers and onions. Cook, stirring occasionally, until the vegetables are softened and slightly caramelized, about 8-10 minutes.
4. Add the minced garlic to the skillet and cook for an additional 1-2 minutes, until fragrant.
5. Return the cooked sausages to the skillet. Stir in the diced tomatoes (with their juices), dried oregano, and dried basil. Season with salt and pepper to taste.
6. Reduce the heat to medium-low and let the mixture simmer for 5-7 minutes, allowing the flavors to meld together.
7. Taste and adjust seasoning if necessary.
8. Garnish with chopped fresh parsley before serving, if desired.
9. Serve the skillet sausage and peppers hot, either on its own or with crusty bread, pasta, rice, or mashed potatoes.

This dish is versatile and can be easily customized to suit your taste preferences. Feel free to add other vegetables such as mushrooms or zucchini, or adjust the level of spiciness by using mild or spicy Italian sausages. Enjoy your delicious skillet sausage and peppers!

Crispy Cast Iron Skillet Chicken Thighs

Ingredients:

- 4-6 bone-in, skin-on chicken thighs
- Salt and pepper to taste
- 1 teaspoon paprika
- 1 teaspoon garlic powder
- 1 teaspoon onion powder
- 1/2 teaspoon dried thyme
- 1/2 teaspoon dried oregano
- 1/2 teaspoon dried rosemary
- 2 tablespoons olive oil or vegetable oil

Instructions:

1. Preheat your oven to 425°F (220°C).
2. Pat the chicken thighs dry with paper towels. This helps to ensure crispy skin.
3. In a small bowl, mix together salt, pepper, paprika, garlic powder, onion powder, dried thyme, dried oregano, and dried rosemary.
4. Season both sides of the chicken thighs generously with the spice mixture.
5. Heat a cast iron skillet over medium-high heat. Once the skillet is hot, add the olive oil.
6. Place the seasoned chicken thighs in the skillet, skin side down. Make sure not to overcrowd the skillet; you may need to cook the thighs in batches.
7. Cook the chicken thighs without moving them for about 5-7 minutes, or until the skin is golden brown and crispy.
8. Flip the chicken thighs using tongs and cook for an additional 2-3 minutes on the other side.
9. Transfer the skillet to the preheated oven and bake for 15-20 minutes, or until the chicken thighs are cooked through and reach an internal temperature of 165°F (74°C).
10. Remove the skillet from the oven and let the chicken thighs rest for a few minutes before serving.
11. Serve the crispy cast iron skillet chicken thighs hot, garnished with fresh herbs if desired.

These crispy chicken thighs are delicious served with mashed potatoes, roasted vegetables, or a simple salad. Enjoy your flavorful and tender chicken thighs straight from the cast iron skillet!

Cast Iron Skillet Cobbler

Ingredients:

For the Fruit Filling:

- 4 cups fresh or frozen fruit (such as peaches, berries, apples, or a combination)
- 1/2 cup granulated sugar (adjust based on the sweetness of the fruit)
- 1 tablespoon cornstarch
- 1 tablespoon lemon juice
- 1 teaspoon vanilla extract
- 1/2 teaspoon ground cinnamon (optional)

For the Cobbler Topping:

- 1 cup all-purpose flour
- 1/2 cup granulated sugar
- 1 teaspoon baking powder
- 1/4 teaspoon salt
- 1/2 cup unsalted butter, melted
- 1/4 cup milk
- 1 teaspoon vanilla extract

Instructions:

1. Preheat your oven to 375°F (190°C).
2. In a large bowl, combine the fruit, sugar, cornstarch, lemon juice, vanilla extract, and ground cinnamon (if using). Toss until the fruit is well coated, then transfer the mixture to a 10-inch cast iron skillet.
3. In another bowl, whisk together the flour, sugar, baking powder, and salt for the cobbler topping.
4. Add the melted butter, milk, and vanilla extract to the dry ingredients. Stir until just combined; the batter will be thick.
5. Drop spoonfuls of the cobbler batter evenly over the fruit mixture in the skillet.
6. Bake the cobbler in the preheated oven for 35-40 minutes, or until the fruit is bubbling and the cobbler topping is golden brown and cooked through.
7. Remove the skillet from the oven and let the cobbler cool slightly before serving.
8. Serve the cast iron skillet cobbler warm, either on its own or with a scoop of vanilla ice cream or whipped cream on top.

Feel free to adjust the type and amount of fruit and spices in the filling based on your preferences and what's in season. You can also sprinkle a little extra sugar over the cobbler topping before baking for added sweetness and crunch. Enjoy your delicious homemade cobbler!

Pan-Seared Scallops

Ingredients:

- 1 pound large sea scallops
- Salt and pepper to taste
- 2 tablespoons unsalted butter
- 2 tablespoons olive oil
- Lemon wedges, for serving
- Fresh parsley, chopped, for garnish (optional)

Instructions:

1. Pat the scallops dry with paper towels. This helps to ensure a good sear.
2. Season both sides of the scallops generously with salt and pepper.
3. Heat the butter and olive oil in a large skillet over medium-high heat. The combination of butter and oil helps prevent the butter from burning.
4. Once the skillet is hot, carefully add the scallops in a single layer, making sure they're not overcrowded. You may need to cook them in batches.
5. Sear the scallops without moving them for about 2-3 minutes, or until the bottoms are golden brown.
6. Using tongs, gently flip the scallops and sear the other side for an additional 2-3 minutes, or until they're cooked through and opaque in the center. Be careful not to overcook them, as scallops can become tough and rubbery if cooked for too long.
7. Remove the scallops from the skillet and transfer them to a serving plate.
8. Squeeze fresh lemon juice over the scallops and garnish with chopped parsley, if desired.
9. Serve the pan-seared scallops hot, accompanied by additional lemon wedges for squeezing over the top.

Pan-seared scallops are delicious served with a side of risotto, pasta, or a fresh salad. Enjoy your elegant and flavorful seafood dish!

Skillet Cornbread with Honey Butter

Ingredients:

For the Skillet Cornbread:

- 1 cup yellow cornmeal
- 1 cup all-purpose flour
- 1 tablespoon baking powder
- 1 teaspoon salt
- 1 cup buttermilk
- 1/4 cup unsalted butter, melted and cooled slightly, plus extra for greasing the skillet
- 1/4 cup granulated sugar
- 2 large eggs

For the Honey Butter:

- 1/2 cup unsalted butter, at room temperature
- 2-3 tablespoons honey, to taste

Instructions:

For the Skillet Cornbread:

1. Preheat your oven to 400°F (200°C). Place a 10-inch cast iron skillet in the oven while it preheats.
2. In a large mixing bowl, whisk together the cornmeal, flour, baking powder, and salt.
3. In another bowl, whisk together the buttermilk, melted butter, sugar, and eggs until well combined.
4. Pour the wet ingredients into the dry ingredients and stir until just combined. Be careful not to overmix; a few lumps are okay.
5. Carefully remove the hot skillet from the oven and grease it with a little butter.
6. Pour the cornbread batter into the hot skillet and spread it out evenly.
7. Bake in the preheated oven for 20-25 minutes, or until the cornbread is golden brown and a toothpick inserted into the center comes out clean.
8. Remove the skillet from the oven and let the cornbread cool slightly before slicing.

For the Honey Butter:

1. In a small bowl, whip the softened butter with a hand mixer until light and fluffy.
2. Gradually add the honey, 1 tablespoon at a time, until the desired sweetness is reached. Taste and adjust as needed.
3. Transfer the honey butter to a serving dish.

To Serve:

1. Slice the warm skillet cornbread into wedges.
2. Serve the cornbread with dollops of honey butter on top or on the side.

3. Enjoy the delicious combination of warm, fluffy cornbread with creamy honey butter!

This skillet cornbread with honey butter makes a wonderful side dish for soups, stews, chili, or barbecue. It's also great on its own as a snack or breakfast treat.

Cast Iron Skillet Tacos

Ingredients:

For the Taco Filling:

- 1 tablespoon olive oil
- 1 small onion, diced
- 2 cloves garlic, minced
- 1 pound ground beef (or your choice of ground meat)
- 1 tablespoon chili powder
- 1 teaspoon ground cumin
- 1/2 teaspoon paprika
- Salt and pepper to taste
- 1/2 cup tomato sauce
- 1/4 cup beef or chicken broth
- 1 cup cooked black beans (optional)
- 1 cup shredded cheese (such as cheddar or Monterey Jack)

For Serving:

- Taco shells or tortillas
- Toppings of your choice: shredded lettuce, diced tomatoes, sliced jalapeños, diced avocado, sour cream, salsa, chopped cilantro, etc.

Instructions:

1. Heat olive oil in a cast iron skillet over medium heat.
2. Add diced onion and minced garlic to the skillet. Cook until softened and fragrant, about 2-3 minutes.
3. Add ground beef to the skillet, breaking it up with a spoon. Cook until browned and no longer pink, about 5-7 minutes.
4. Stir in chili powder, ground cumin, paprika, salt, and pepper. Cook for another 1-2 minutes until spices are fragrant.
5. Pour in tomato sauce and beef or chicken broth. Stir to combine. If using black beans, add them to the skillet as well.
6. Simmer the taco filling for 5-7 minutes, stirring occasionally, until the sauce has thickened slightly.
7. Sprinkle shredded cheese over the taco filling. Cover the skillet and let the cheese melt for 2-3 minutes.
8. While the cheese is melting, warm up your taco shells or tortillas according to package instructions.
9. Once the cheese has melted, remove the skillet from heat.
10. Serve the skillet tacos hot with warmed taco shells or tortillas and your choice of toppings.
11. Let everyone assemble their own tacos with their favorite toppings.

These cast iron skillet tacos are customizable and perfect for a crowd. They make a great weeknight dinner or a fun meal for entertaining guests. Enjoy!

Spinach and Feta Frittata

Ingredients:

- 8 large eggs
- 1/4 cup milk or heavy cream
- Salt and pepper to taste
- 2 tablespoons olive oil
- 1 small onion, diced
- 2 cloves garlic, minced
- 2 cups fresh spinach leaves, chopped
- 1/2 cup crumbled feta cheese
- Optional: chopped fresh herbs such as parsley or dill

Instructions:

1. Preheat your oven to 350°F (175°C).
2. In a large mixing bowl, whisk together the eggs, milk or cream, salt, and pepper until well combined. Set aside.
3. Heat olive oil in an oven-safe skillet (preferably cast iron) over medium heat.
4. Add diced onion and minced garlic to the skillet. Sauté until softened and fragrant, about 2-3 minutes.
5. Add chopped spinach to the skillet and cook until wilted, about 2-3 minutes more.
6. Spread the spinach and onion mixture evenly in the skillet.
7. Pour the whisked egg mixture over the spinach mixture in the skillet. Gently shake the skillet to distribute the eggs evenly.
8. Sprinkle crumbled feta cheese over the top of the egg mixture.
9. Cook the frittata on the stovetop for 3-4 minutes, until the edges start to set.
10. Transfer the skillet to the preheated oven and bake for 12-15 minutes, or until the frittata is set in the center and lightly golden on top.
11. Once cooked, remove the skillet from the oven and let the frittata cool slightly.
12. Sprinkle chopped fresh herbs over the frittata, if using.
13. Slice the frittata into wedges and serve warm or at room temperature.

This Spinach and Feta Frittata is delicious on its own or served with a side salad, crusty bread, or roasted potatoes. It's a versatile dish that's perfect for any meal of the day!

Skillet Pork Tenderloin with Mustard Sauce

Ingredients:

For the Pork Tenderloin:

- 2 pork tenderloins (about 1 to 1.5 pounds each)
- Salt and pepper to taste
- 2 tablespoons olive oil or vegetable oil
- 2 cloves garlic, minced
- 1 teaspoon dried thyme
- 1 teaspoon dried rosemary

For the Mustard Sauce:

- 2 tablespoons unsalted butter
- 2 tablespoons all-purpose flour
- 1 cup chicken broth
- 1/4 cup Dijon mustard
- 2 tablespoons whole grain mustard
- 2 tablespoons honey
- Salt and pepper to taste
- Chopped fresh parsley, for garnish (optional)

Instructions:

For the Pork Tenderloin:

1. Preheat your oven to 375°F (190°C).
2. Pat the pork tenderloins dry with paper towels. Season them generously with salt and pepper on all sides.
3. Heat the olive oil in a large oven-safe skillet over medium-high heat.
4. Once the skillet is hot, add the pork tenderloins to the skillet. Sear them on all sides until browned, about 2-3 minutes per side.
5. Add minced garlic, dried thyme, and dried rosemary to the skillet. Stir and cook for about 1 minute until fragrant.
6. Transfer the skillet to the preheated oven and roast the pork tenderloins for 15-20 minutes, or until they reach an internal temperature of 145°F (63°C). Use a meat thermometer to check for doneness.
7. Once cooked, remove the skillet from the oven and transfer the pork tenderloins to a cutting board. Let them rest for 5-10 minutes before slicing.

For the Mustard Sauce:

1. While the pork tenderloins are resting, make the mustard sauce.
2. In the same skillet used to cook the pork, melt the butter over medium heat.
3. Stir in the flour and cook for 1-2 minutes, until the mixture is smooth and bubbly.

4. Gradually whisk in the chicken broth, stirring constantly to prevent lumps from forming.
5. Add the Dijon mustard, whole grain mustard, and honey to the skillet. Stir to combine.
6. Simmer the sauce for 3-5 minutes, or until it thickens to your desired consistency. Season with salt and pepper to taste.
7. Remove the skillet from the heat.

To Serve:

1. Slice the rested pork tenderloins into medallions.
2. Serve the sliced pork tenderloin with the mustard sauce spooned over the top.
3. Garnish with chopped fresh parsley, if desired.
4. Serve immediately and enjoy your skillet pork tenderloin with mustard sauce!

This dish pairs well with roasted vegetables, mashed potatoes, or a green salad. It's sure to impress your family and guests!

Cast Iron Skillet Cinnamon Rolls

Ingredients:

For the Dough:

- 4 cups all-purpose flour
- 1/4 cup granulated sugar
- 1 teaspoon salt
- 2 1/4 teaspoons active dry yeast (1 packet)
- 1 cup warm milk (110°F/45°C)
- 1/4 cup unsalted butter, melted
- 2 large eggs

For the Filling:

- 1/2 cup unsalted butter, softened
- 1 cup brown sugar, packed
- 2 tablespoons ground cinnamon

For the Cream Cheese Glaze:

- 4 ounces cream cheese, softened
- 1/4 cup unsalted butter, softened
- 1 cup powdered sugar
- 1 teaspoon vanilla extract
- 2-3 tablespoons milk

Instructions:

For the Dough:

1. In a large mixing bowl, combine the warm milk and yeast. Let it sit for about 5 minutes until foamy.
2. Add melted butter, sugar, salt, and eggs to the yeast mixture. Mix well.
3. Gradually add flour, stirring until a dough forms.
4. Knead the dough on a lightly floured surface for about 5-7 minutes until smooth and elastic.
5. Place the dough in a greased bowl, cover with a clean kitchen towel, and let it rise in a warm place for about 1 hour, or until doubled in size.

For the Filling:

1. In a small bowl, mix together softened butter, brown sugar, and ground cinnamon until well combined.

Assembly:

1. Punch down the risen dough and transfer it to a floured surface.
2. Roll out the dough into a rectangle, about 1/4 inch thick.
3. Spread the filling evenly over the dough, leaving a small border around the edges.
4. Starting from one long side, tightly roll up the dough into a log.
5. Cut the dough into 12 equal-sized rolls using a sharp knife or a piece of unflavored dental floss.
6. Grease a 12-inch cast iron skillet with butter and arrange the cinnamon rolls in the skillet, leaving a little space between each roll.
7. Cover the skillet with a clean kitchen towel and let the rolls rise in a warm place for about 30-45 minutes, or until puffy.

Baking:

1. Preheat your oven to 350°F (175°C).
2. Once the rolls have risen, bake them in the preheated oven for 25-30 minutes, or until golden brown.
3. Remove the skillet from the oven and let the cinnamon rolls cool slightly.

For the Cream Cheese Glaze:

1. In a mixing bowl, beat together softened cream cheese and butter until smooth.
2. Gradually add powdered sugar and vanilla extract, mixing until creamy.
3. Add milk, one tablespoon at a time, until the glaze reaches your desired consistency.
4. Drizzle the glaze over the warm cinnamon rolls in the skillet.
5. Serve the cast iron skillet cinnamon rolls warm and enjoy!

These cinnamon rolls are best served fresh from the oven. They're perfect for breakfast, brunch, or as a sweet treat any time of the day.

Skillet Shepherd's Pie

Ingredients:

For the Filling:

- 1 tablespoon olive oil
- 1 onion, diced
- 2 cloves garlic, minced
- 1 pound ground beef or lamb
- 2 carrots, diced
- 1 cup frozen peas
- 2 tablespoons tomato paste
- 1 tablespoon Worcestershire sauce
- 1 teaspoon dried thyme
- Salt and pepper to taste
- 1 cup beef or vegetable broth
- 2 tablespoons all-purpose flour
- 2 tablespoons chopped fresh parsley (optional)

For the Mashed Potato Topping:

- 2 pounds potatoes, peeled and cut into chunks
- 1/4 cup unsalted butter
- 1/2 cup milk or cream
- Salt and pepper to taste
- 1/2 cup shredded cheddar cheese (optional)

Instructions:

For the Filling:

1. Heat olive oil in a large oven-safe skillet over medium heat.
2. Add diced onion and minced garlic to the skillet. Sauté until softened and fragrant, about 2-3 minutes.
3. Add ground beef or lamb to the skillet. Cook until browned, breaking it up with a spoon.
4. Stir in diced carrots and frozen peas. Cook for another 3-4 minutes until vegetables start to soften.
5. Add tomato paste, Worcestershire sauce, dried thyme, salt, and pepper to the skillet. Stir to combine.
6. Sprinkle flour over the meat and vegetable mixture. Cook for 1-2 minutes, stirring constantly.
7. Gradually pour in beef or vegetable broth, stirring constantly to avoid lumps. Bring to a simmer and cook until the mixture thickens, about 3-5 minutes.
8. Remove the skillet from heat and stir in chopped fresh parsley, if using.

For the Mashed Potato Topping:

1. Place peeled and chopped potatoes in a large pot of salted water. Bring to a boil and cook until potatoes are fork-tender, about 15-20 minutes.
2. Drain the cooked potatoes and return them to the pot.
3. Add butter, milk or cream, salt, and pepper to the pot with the cooked potatoes. Mash until smooth and creamy.

Assembly and Baking:

1. Preheat your oven to 400°F (200°C).
2. Spoon the mashed potatoes over the filling in the skillet, spreading them out evenly.
3. If desired, sprinkle shredded cheddar cheese over the mashed potatoes.
4. Place the skillet in the preheated oven and bake for 20-25 minutes, or until the mashed potatoes are lightly golden and the filling is bubbly.
5. Remove the skillet from the oven and let it cool for a few minutes before serving.

Enjoy your delicious skillet shepherd's pie straight from the oven! It's a complete meal in one dish, perfect for sharing with family and friends.

One-Pot Jambalaya

Ingredients:

- 1 tablespoon olive oil
- 1 pound chicken thighs, boneless and skinless, cut into bite-sized pieces
- 1 pound smoked sausage (such as Andouille), sliced
- 1 onion, diced
- 1 bell pepper, diced
- 2 celery stalks, diced
- 3 cloves garlic, minced
- 1 can (14.5 ounces) diced tomatoes
- 1 cup long-grain white rice
- 2 cups chicken broth
- 2 teaspoons Cajun seasoning
- 1 teaspoon dried thyme
- 1 teaspoon paprika
- 1/2 teaspoon cayenne pepper (optional, adjust to taste)
- Salt and pepper to taste
- 1 cup frozen okra (optional)
- 1 cup peeled and deveined shrimp (optional)
- Chopped fresh parsley, for garnish

Instructions:

1. Heat olive oil in a large Dutch oven or heavy-bottomed pot over medium-high heat.
2. Add the chicken pieces to the pot and cook until browned on all sides, about 5 minutes. Remove from the pot and set aside.
3. Add the sliced sausage to the pot and cook until browned, about 3-4 minutes. Remove from the pot and set aside with the chicken.
4. In the same pot, add diced onion, bell pepper, and celery. Cook until softened, about 5 minutes.
5. Add minced garlic to the pot and cook for an additional minute until fragrant.
6. Stir in diced tomatoes (with their juices), rice, chicken broth, Cajun seasoning, dried thyme, paprika, cayenne pepper (if using), salt, and pepper.
7. Bring the mixture to a boil, then reduce the heat to low and cover the pot. Let it simmer for 15-20 minutes, or until the rice is cooked and most of the liquid is absorbed.
8. If using frozen okra, add it to the pot during the last 5 minutes of cooking.
9. If using shrimp, stir in the peeled and deveined shrimp during the last 5 minutes of cooking, until they turn pink and opaque.
10. Once the rice is cooked and the shrimp (if using) are cooked through, return the cooked chicken and sausage to the pot. Stir to combine and heat through.
11. Taste and adjust seasoning if necessary.
12. Garnish the Jambalaya with chopped fresh parsley before serving.

Enjoy your flavorful one-pot Jambalaya hot, garnished with parsley for freshness. It's a complete meal packed with Cajun-inspired flavors that the whole family will love!

Lemon Herb Roast Chicken

Ingredients:

- 1 whole chicken (about 4-5 pounds)
- Salt and pepper to taste
- 2 lemons, halved
- 4 cloves garlic, minced
- 2 tablespoons olive oil
- 2 tablespoons fresh herbs (such as rosemary, thyme, and parsley), chopped
- 1 onion, quartered
- 2 carrots, chopped
- 2 celery stalks, chopped
- 1 cup chicken broth or water

Instructions:

1. Preheat your oven to 425°F (220°C).
2. Pat the whole chicken dry with paper towels. This helps to ensure crispy skin.
3. Season the chicken generously inside and out with salt and pepper.
4. Squeeze the juice of one lemon all over the chicken, then place the lemon halves inside the cavity.
5. In a small bowl, mix together the minced garlic, olive oil, and chopped herbs. Rub this mixture all over the chicken, ensuring it's evenly coated.
6. Place the quartered onion, chopped carrots, and celery in the bottom of a roasting pan or a large oven-safe skillet.
7. Place the seasoned chicken on top of the vegetables in the pan or skillet.
8. Pour the chicken broth or water into the bottom of the pan.
9. Place the pan or skillet in the preheated oven and roast the chicken for about 1 hour and 15 minutes to 1 hour and 30 minutes, or until the internal temperature reaches 165°F (75°C) in the thickest part of the thigh and the juices run clear.
10. If the skin starts to brown too quickly, you can cover the chicken loosely with aluminum foil.
11. Once the chicken is cooked through, remove it from the oven and let it rest for about 10-15 minutes before carving.
12. Serve the lemon herb roast chicken with the roasted vegetables and pan juices.

Enjoy your delicious and aromatic lemon herb roast chicken with your favorite sides, such as mashed potatoes, roasted vegetables, or a fresh salad. It's perfect for a special dinner or a comforting Sunday meal with the family!

Cast Iron Skillet Biscuits and Gravy

Ingredients:

For the Biscuits:

- 2 cups all-purpose flour
- 1 tablespoon baking powder
- 1 teaspoon salt
- 1/2 cup unsalted butter, cold and cut into cubes
- 3/4 cup buttermilk

For the Gravy:

- 1/2 pound breakfast sausage (pork or turkey)
- 2 tablespoons unsalted butter
- 1/4 cup all-purpose flour
- 2 cups whole milk
- Salt and pepper to taste

Instructions:

For the Biscuits:

1. Preheat your oven to 425°F (220°C).
2. In a large mixing bowl, whisk together the flour, baking powder, and salt.
3. Add the cold butter cubes to the flour mixture. Using a pastry cutter or your fingers, work the butter into the flour until the mixture resembles coarse crumbs.
4. Gradually pour in the buttermilk, stirring with a fork, until the dough comes together. Be careful not to overmix.
5. Turn the dough out onto a floured surface. Gently pat or roll out the dough to about 1-inch thickness.
6. Use a biscuit cutter or the rim of a glass to cut out biscuits. Place the biscuits in a greased cast iron skillet, fitting them snugly together.
7. Bake the biscuits in the preheated oven for 12-15 minutes, or until golden brown and cooked through.

For the Gravy:

1. While the biscuits are baking, cook the breakfast sausage in a large skillet over medium heat, breaking it up into crumbles as it cooks. Once browned and cooked through, remove the sausage from the skillet and set aside.
2. In the same skillet, melt the butter over medium heat.
3. Gradually whisk in the flour to form a roux. Cook the roux, stirring constantly, for 1-2 minutes until golden brown.
4. Slowly pour in the milk, whisking constantly to prevent lumps from forming.

5. Cook the gravy, stirring frequently, until it thickens to your desired consistency, about 5-7 minutes.
6. Season the gravy with salt and pepper to taste.
7. Stir the cooked breakfast sausage back into the gravy, heating it through.

To Serve:

1. Split the warm biscuits in half and place them on serving plates or a large platter.
2. Spoon the sausage gravy over the biscuits.
3. Garnish with chopped fresh parsley or a sprinkle of black pepper, if desired.
4. Serve the cast iron skillet biscuits and gravy hot, and enjoy!

This classic breakfast dish is sure to be a hit with family and friends. It's perfect for a weekend brunch or any time you're craving a comforting meal.

Skillet Beef Stir-Fry

Ingredients:

- 1 pound beef sirloin or flank steak, thinly sliced against the grain
- 2 tablespoons soy sauce
- 1 tablespoon oyster sauce
- 1 tablespoon hoisin sauce
- 2 teaspoons cornstarch
- 2 tablespoons vegetable oil, divided
- 3 cloves garlic, minced
- 1 tablespoon minced ginger
- 1 onion, thinly sliced
- 2 bell peppers, thinly sliced
- 1 cup broccoli florets
- 1 cup sliced mushrooms
- Salt and pepper to taste
- Cooked rice or noodles, for serving
- Chopped green onions and sesame seeds for garnish (optional)

Instructions:

1. In a bowl, combine the soy sauce, oyster sauce, hoisin sauce, and cornstarch. Add the sliced beef to the bowl and toss until well coated. Let it marinate for about 15-30 minutes.
2. Heat 1 tablespoon of vegetable oil in a large skillet or wok over medium-high heat.
3. Add the marinated beef to the skillet and cook, stirring frequently, until browned and cooked through, about 3-4 minutes. Remove the beef from the skillet and set aside.
4. In the same skillet, add the remaining tablespoon of vegetable oil.
5. Add the minced garlic and ginger to the skillet and cook for about 30 seconds, until fragrant.
6. Add the sliced onion, bell peppers, broccoli florets, and mushrooms to the skillet. Cook, stirring constantly, until the vegetables are tender-crisp, about 3-4 minutes.
7. Return the cooked beef to the skillet and stir to combine with the vegetables.
8. Season the stir-fry with salt and pepper to taste.
9. Serve the skillet beef stir-fry hot over cooked rice or noodles.
10. Garnish with chopped green onions and sesame seeds, if desired.

Enjoy your delicious skillet beef stir-fry packed with tender beef, crisp vegetables, and flavorful sauce. It's a satisfying and nutritious meal that's ready in no time!

Cast Iron Skillet Gooey Butter Cake

Ingredients:

For the Cake:

- 1 package (18.25 ounces) yellow cake mix
- 1/2 cup unsalted butter, melted
- 2 large eggs

For the Gooey Butter Layer:

- 1 package (8 ounces) cream cheese, softened
- 2 large eggs
- 1 teaspoon vanilla extract
- 1/2 cup unsalted butter, melted
- 2 cups powdered sugar, sifted, plus extra for dusting

Instructions:

1. Preheat your oven to 350°F (175°C). Grease a 10-inch cast iron skillet with butter or cooking spray.
2. In a large mixing bowl, combine the yellow cake mix, melted butter, and eggs. Mix until well combined.
3. Press the cake mixture evenly into the bottom of the prepared cast iron skillet, creating a crust layer.
4. In another mixing bowl, beat the softened cream cheese until smooth.
5. Add the eggs, one at a time, beating well after each addition.
6. Mix in the vanilla extract and melted butter until smooth.
7. Gradually add the sifted powdered sugar, beating until well combined and smooth.
8. Pour the cream cheese mixture over the cake mixture in the skillet, spreading it out evenly.
9. Bake in the preheated oven for 35-40 minutes, or until the edges are golden brown and the center is set but still slightly jiggly.
10. Remove the skillet from the oven and let the cake cool in the skillet for at least 30 minutes.
11. Once cooled, dust the top of the cake with powdered sugar.
12. Slice the Gooey Butter Cake into wedges and serve.

Enjoy your delicious Cast Iron Skillet Gooey Butter Cake as a rich and indulgent dessert. It's perfect for sharing with family and friends on special occasions or any time you're craving something sweet!

Skillet Chicken Enchiladas

Ingredients:

For the Enchilada Sauce:

- 2 tablespoons olive oil
- 2 tablespoons all-purpose flour
- 2 tablespoons chili powder
- 1 teaspoon ground cumin
- 1/2 teaspoon garlic powder
- 1/4 teaspoon dried oregano
- 2 cups chicken broth
- Salt and pepper to taste

For the Enchiladas:

- 1 tablespoon olive oil
- 1 small onion, diced
- 2 cloves garlic, minced
- 1 pound boneless, skinless chicken breasts, diced
- Salt and pepper to taste
- 1 can (15 ounces) black beans, drained and rinsed
- 1 can (4 ounces) diced green chilies
- 1 cup frozen corn kernels
- 8-10 small corn or flour tortillas
- 2 cups shredded cheese (such as cheddar or Monterey Jack)
- Optional toppings: diced tomatoes, sliced jalapeños, chopped cilantro, sour cream, avocado slices, etc.

Instructions:

For the Enchilada Sauce:

1. In a medium saucepan, heat the olive oil over medium heat.
2. Add the flour, chili powder, cumin, garlic powder, and dried oregano to the saucepan. Cook, stirring constantly, for 1-2 minutes to toast the spices.
3. Gradually whisk in the chicken broth until smooth. Bring the sauce to a simmer and cook for 5-7 minutes, stirring occasionally, until thickened.
4. Season the enchilada sauce with salt and pepper to taste. Remove from heat and set aside.

For the Enchiladas:

1. Preheat your oven to 375°F (190°C).

2. Heat olive oil in a large oven-safe skillet over medium heat.
3. Add diced onion and minced garlic to the skillet. Cook until softened and fragrant, about 2-3 minutes.
4. Season the diced chicken breasts with salt and pepper, then add them to the skillet. Cook until browned and cooked through, about 5-7 minutes.
5. Stir in the black beans, diced green chilies, and frozen corn kernels. Cook for an additional 2-3 minutes to heat through.
6. Pour about 1 cup of the prepared enchilada sauce over the chicken mixture in the skillet, reserving the remaining sauce for serving.
7. Arrange the tortillas over the top of the chicken mixture in the skillet, overlapping slightly if needed.
8. Sprinkle shredded cheese evenly over the top of the tortillas.
9. Transfer the skillet to the preheated oven and bake for 15-20 minutes, or until the cheese is melted and bubbly.
10. Remove the skillet from the oven and let it cool for a few minutes before serving.
11. Serve the skillet chicken enchiladas hot, garnished with your favorite toppings and with the reserved enchilada sauce on the side.

Enjoy your delicious skillet chicken enchiladas, packed with flavorful chicken, beans, and cheese, all cooked in one skillet for easy cleanup!

Cast Iron Skillet Caramelized Onion Dip

Ingredients:

- 2 large onions, thinly sliced
- 2 tablespoons unsalted butter
- 1 tablespoon olive oil
- 1 teaspoon brown sugar
- 1/2 teaspoon salt
- 1/4 teaspoon black pepper
- 1 cup sour cream
- 1/2 cup mayonnaise
- 1/2 cup grated Parmesan cheese
- 1/4 cup chopped fresh chives (optional)
- Salt and pepper to taste
- Crackers, bread, or vegetables for serving

Instructions:

1. Heat a large cast iron skillet over medium heat. Add the butter and olive oil to the skillet.
2. Once the butter has melted, add the sliced onions to the skillet. Cook, stirring occasionally, for about 30-40 minutes, or until the onions are caramelized and golden brown.
3. Sprinkle brown sugar, salt, and black pepper over the caramelized onions and stir to combine. Cook for an additional 2-3 minutes.
4. Preheat your oven to 375°F (190°C).
5. In a mixing bowl, combine sour cream, mayonnaise, grated Parmesan cheese, and chopped fresh chives (if using). Stir until well combined.
6. Add the caramelized onions to the sour cream mixture and stir to combine. Season with salt and pepper to taste.
7. Transfer the onion dip mixture back to the cast iron skillet, spreading it out evenly.
8. Bake in the preheated oven for 20-25 minutes, or until the dip is hot and bubbly.
9. If desired, broil the dip for an additional 1-2 minutes to brown the top.
10. Remove the skillet from the oven and let the dip cool for a few minutes before serving.
11. Serve the cast iron skillet caramelized onion dip hot, alongside crackers, bread, or vegetables for dipping.

Enjoy your delicious caramelized onion dip, packed with sweet caramelized onions and savory cheese, served straight from the cast iron skillet for a rustic presentation. It's sure to be a hit at any party or gathering!

Skillet Ratatouille

Ingredients:

- 2 tablespoons olive oil
- 1 onion, diced
- 2 cloves garlic, minced
- 1 eggplant, diced
- 2 zucchini, diced
- 2 bell peppers (red, yellow, or orange), diced
- 2 tomatoes, diced
- 1 can (14 ounces) diced tomatoes, undrained
- 1 teaspoon dried thyme
- 1 teaspoon dried oregano
- Salt and pepper to taste
- Fresh basil leaves, chopped, for garnish

Instructions:

1. Heat olive oil in a large skillet over medium heat.
2. Add diced onion to the skillet and cook until softened, about 2-3 minutes.
3. Add minced garlic to the skillet and cook for an additional minute until fragrant.
4. Add diced eggplant, zucchini, and bell peppers to the skillet. Cook, stirring occasionally, for about 5 minutes until the vegetables start to soften.
5. Stir in diced fresh tomatoes, canned diced tomatoes (with their juices), dried thyme, dried oregano, salt, and pepper. Mix well to combine.
6. Reduce the heat to low, cover the skillet, and let the ratatouille simmer for 15-20 minutes, stirring occasionally, until the vegetables are tender and the flavors have melded together.
7. Taste and adjust seasoning if necessary.
8. Garnish the skillet ratatouille with chopped fresh basil leaves before serving.

Enjoy your delicious skillet ratatouille as a flavorful side dish or main course. It's perfect served over cooked pasta, rice, or crusty bread, and makes a satisfying and nutritious meal!

Cast Iron Skillet Blueberry Pancakes

Ingredients:

- 1 cup all-purpose flour
- 2 tablespoons granulated sugar
- 1 teaspoon baking powder
- 1/2 teaspoon baking soda
- 1/4 teaspoon salt
- 1 cup buttermilk
- 1 large egg
- 2 tablespoons unsalted butter, melted
- 1 teaspoon vanilla extract
- 1/2 cup fresh or frozen blueberries
- Butter or oil for greasing the skillet

Instructions:

1. In a large mixing bowl, whisk together the flour, sugar, baking powder, baking soda, and salt.
2. In a separate bowl, whisk together the buttermilk, egg, melted butter, and vanilla extract until well combined.
3. Pour the wet ingredients into the dry ingredients and stir until just combined. Be careful not to overmix; a few lumps are okay.
4. Gently fold in the blueberries until evenly distributed throughout the batter.
5. Place a cast iron skillet over medium heat and grease it lightly with butter or oil.
6. Once the skillet is hot, pour about 1/4 cup of the pancake batter onto the skillet for each pancake, spacing them apart.
7. Cook the pancakes for 2-3 minutes, or until bubbles form on the surface and the edges look set.
8. Carefully flip the pancakes with a spatula and cook for an additional 1-2 minutes, or until golden brown and cooked through.
9. Transfer the cooked pancakes to a plate and keep warm while you cook the remaining batter, greasing the skillet as needed between batches.
10. Serve the blueberry pancakes warm with your favorite toppings, such as maple syrup, extra blueberries, whipped cream, or butter.

Enjoy your delicious cast iron skillet blueberry pancakes for a delightful breakfast or brunch treat!

Shrimp and Grits

Ingredients:

For the Shrimp:

- 1 pound large shrimp, peeled and deveined
- 2 cloves garlic, minced
- 2 tablespoons unsalted butter
- 1 tablespoon olive oil
- 1 teaspoon Cajun seasoning (or to taste)
- Salt and pepper to taste
- 2 tablespoons chopped fresh parsley

For the Grits:

- 1 cup stone-ground grits
- 4 cups water or chicken broth
- 1 cup milk
- 2 tablespoons unsalted butter
- Salt and pepper to taste
- 1 cup shredded cheddar cheese (optional)

For Serving:

- Crumbled cooked bacon (optional)
- Sliced green onions (optional)
- Hot sauce (optional)

Instructions:

For the Shrimp:

1. Pat the shrimp dry with paper towels and season them with Cajun seasoning, salt, and pepper.
2. Heat the butter and olive oil in a large skillet over medium-high heat.
3. Add the minced garlic to the skillet and cook for about 30 seconds, until fragrant.
4. Add the seasoned shrimp to the skillet in a single layer. Cook for 2-3 minutes per side, or until they are pink and opaque.
5. Stir in the chopped parsley and remove the skillet from the heat. Set aside.

For the Grits:

1. In a large saucepan, bring the water or chicken broth to a boil.
2. Gradually whisk in the stone-ground grits, stirring constantly to prevent lumps from forming.

3. Reduce the heat to low and simmer, stirring occasionally, for about 20-25 minutes, or until the grits are thick and creamy.
4. Stir in the milk, butter, and shredded cheddar cheese (if using) until the cheese is melted and the grits are smooth.
5. Season the grits with salt and pepper to taste.

To Serve:

1. Divide the creamy grits among serving bowls.
2. Top the grits with the cooked shrimp and any pan juices from the skillet.
3. Garnish with crumbled cooked bacon, sliced green onions, and hot sauce, if desired.
4. Serve the shrimp and grits immediately, while hot.

Enjoy your delicious shrimp and grits, a classic Southern comfort food that's perfect for any meal of the day!

Skillet Beef and Broccoli

Ingredients:

- 1 pound flank steak or sirloin steak, thinly sliced against the grain
- 1/4 cup soy sauce
- 2 tablespoons oyster sauce
- 2 tablespoons brown sugar
- 2 cloves garlic, minced
- 1 teaspoon fresh ginger, grated
- 2 tablespoons vegetable oil, divided
- 1 head broccoli, cut into florets
- 1/2 cup beef broth or water
- 1 tablespoon cornstarch
- Cooked rice, for serving
- Sesame seeds and sliced green onions, for garnish (optional)

Instructions:

1. In a bowl, combine the soy sauce, oyster sauce, brown sugar, minced garlic, and grated ginger. Add the thinly sliced beef to the bowl and toss to coat. Let it marinate for at least 15 minutes.
2. Heat 1 tablespoon of vegetable oil in a large skillet over medium-high heat. Add the marinated beef to the skillet and cook for 2-3 minutes, stirring occasionally, until browned. Remove the beef from the skillet and set aside.
3. In the same skillet, add the remaining tablespoon of vegetable oil. Add the broccoli florets to the skillet and sauté for 3-4 minutes, or until they are bright green and tender-crisp.
4. In a small bowl, whisk together the beef broth (or water) and cornstarch until smooth. Pour the mixture into the skillet with the broccoli.
5. Return the cooked beef to the skillet and stir to combine with the broccoli.
6. Cook for an additional 1-2 minutes, or until the sauce has thickened and the beef is heated through.
7. Serve the skillet beef and broccoli hot over cooked rice.
8. Garnish with sesame seeds and sliced green onions, if desired.

Enjoy your delicious skillet beef and broccoli, served with tender beef and crisp broccoli in a flavorful sauce. It's a satisfying and nutritious meal that's ready in no time!

Cast Iron Skillet Chocolate Chip Cookie

Ingredients:

- 1/2 cup unsalted butter, melted
- 1/2 cup granulated sugar
- 1/2 cup packed light brown sugar
- 1 large egg
- 1 teaspoon vanilla extract
- 1 and 1/2 cups all-purpose flour
- 1/2 teaspoon baking soda
- 1/2 teaspoon salt
- 1 cup semisweet chocolate chips

Instructions:

1. Preheat your oven to 350°F (175°C).
2. In a large mixing bowl, whisk together the melted butter, granulated sugar, and brown sugar until well combined.
3. Add the egg and vanilla extract to the bowl and whisk until smooth.
4. In a separate bowl, sift together the all-purpose flour, baking soda, and salt.
5. Gradually add the dry ingredients to the wet ingredients, stirring with a wooden spoon or spatula until just combined.
6. Fold in the semisweet chocolate chips until evenly distributed throughout the cookie dough.
7. Transfer the cookie dough to a greased 10-inch cast iron skillet, spreading it out evenly.
8. Bake in the preheated oven for 20-25 minutes, or until the edges are golden brown and the center is set.
9. Remove the skillet from the oven and let the cookie cool in the skillet for at least 10 minutes before slicing and serving.

Enjoy your delicious cast iron skillet chocolate chip cookie, served warm with a scoop of vanilla ice cream for an extra indulgent treat!

Skillet Corned Beef Hash

Ingredients:

- 2 tablespoons unsalted butter
- 1 onion, diced
- 2 cloves garlic, minced
- 2 cups cooked corned beef, diced
- 3 cups cooked potatoes, diced (leftover boiled or roasted potatoes work well)
- Salt and pepper to taste
- 1/2 teaspoon paprika
- 1/4 teaspoon dried thyme
- 1/4 teaspoon dried parsley
- Optional: chopped fresh parsley or green onions for garnish
- Optional: eggs, cooked sunny-side up or poached, for serving

Instructions:

1. In a large skillet, melt the butter over medium heat.
2. Add the diced onion to the skillet and cook until softened and translucent, about 5 minutes.
3. Add the minced garlic to the skillet and cook for an additional 1-2 minutes, until fragrant.
4. Add the diced corned beef and potatoes to the skillet, spreading them out into an even layer.
5. Season the mixture with salt, pepper, paprika, dried thyme, and dried parsley. Stir to combine.
6. Allow the corned beef hash to cook undisturbed for about 5-7 minutes, until the bottom is browned and crispy.
7. Using a spatula, flip sections of the hash over to brown the other side. Cook for an additional 5-7 minutes, until the other side is browned and crispy.
8. Once the hash is cooked to your liking, remove the skillet from the heat.
9. Serve the skillet corned beef hash hot, garnished with chopped fresh parsley or green onions if desired.
10. Optionally, serve with cooked eggs on top, such as sunny-side up or poached eggs.

Enjoy your delicious skillet corned beef hash as a satisfying and flavorful breakfast or brunch dish! It pairs well with eggs and toast for a complete meal.

Cast Iron Skillet BBQ Ribs

Ingredients:

- 2 racks of baby back ribs
- Salt and pepper to taste
- 1 cup BBQ sauce of your choice
- 1/4 cup apple cider vinegar
- 1/4 cup brown sugar
- 1 tablespoon Worcestershire sauce
- 1 teaspoon smoked paprika
- 1/2 teaspoon garlic powder
- 1/2 teaspoon onion powder
- 1/4 teaspoon cayenne pepper (optional, for heat)
- Vegetable oil for greasing the skillet

Instructions:

1. Preheat your oven to 300°F (150°C).
2. Season the racks of baby back ribs generously with salt and pepper on both sides.
3. In a small bowl, whisk together the BBQ sauce, apple cider vinegar, brown sugar, Worcestershire sauce, smoked paprika, garlic powder, onion powder, and cayenne pepper (if using) to make the BBQ glaze.
4. Place the seasoned ribs in a large roasting pan or baking dish, meaty side up.
5. Pour half of the BBQ glaze over the ribs, spreading it out evenly to coat.
6. Cover the roasting pan or baking dish tightly with aluminum foil.
7. Transfer the covered roasting pan or baking dish to the preheated oven and bake for 2 to 2 1/2 hours, or until the ribs are tender and cooked through.
8. Remove the foil from the roasting pan or baking dish and carefully drain any excess liquid.
9. Heat a cast iron skillet over medium-high heat. Lightly grease the skillet with vegetable oil.
10. Transfer the partially cooked ribs to the greased cast iron skillet, arranging them in a single layer.
11. Brush the remaining BBQ glaze over the tops of the ribs, reserving some for basting.
12. Place the cast iron skillet in the oven under the broiler for 3-5 minutes, or until the glaze is caramelized and bubbly, watching closely to prevent burning.
13. Carefully remove the skillet from the oven and turn the ribs over. Brush with additional BBQ glaze.
14. Return the skillet to the broiler for another 3-5 minutes, or until the glaze is caramelized and bubbly on the other side.
15. Remove the skillet from the oven and let the ribs rest for a few minutes before serving.

Enjoy your delicious cast iron skillet BBQ ribs, served hot with your favorite sides, such as coleslaw, baked beans, or cornbread, for a hearty and satisfying meal!

Skillet Lemon Garlic Butter Salmon

Ingredients:

- 4 salmon fillets (about 6 ounces each), skin-on or skinless
- Salt and pepper to taste
- 2 tablespoons unsalted butter
- 2 cloves garlic, minced
- Zest of 1 lemon
- Juice of 1 lemon
- 2 tablespoons chopped fresh parsley
- Lemon slices for garnish (optional)

Instructions:

1. Season the salmon fillets with salt and pepper on both sides.
2. In a large skillet, melt the butter over medium heat.
3. Add the minced garlic to the skillet and cook for about 1 minute, until fragrant.
4. Place the seasoned salmon fillets in the skillet, skin-side down if using skin-on fillets.
5. Cook the salmon for 4-5 minutes on each side, depending on thickness, until golden brown and cooked to your desired level of doneness. Use a spatula to carefully flip the salmon halfway through cooking.
6. While the salmon is cooking, sprinkle lemon zest over the fillets and squeeze lemon juice over them.
7. Spoon some of the melted butter and garlic mixture over the salmon as it cooks.
8. Once the salmon is cooked through, sprinkle chopped fresh parsley over the top for garnish.
9. Serve the skillet lemon garlic butter salmon hot, garnished with lemon slices if desired.

Enjoy your delicious skillet lemon garlic butter salmon, served with your favorite sides such as roasted vegetables, rice, or salad, for a flavorful and healthy meal!

Cast Iron Skillet French Toast

Ingredients:

- 4 slices of bread (thick slices work best, such as brioche or challah)
- 2 large eggs
- 1/2 cup milk
- 1 teaspoon vanilla extract
- 1/2 teaspoon ground cinnamon
- 1 tablespoon unsalted butter
- Maple syrup, powdered sugar, fresh berries, or sliced fruit for serving (optional)

Instructions:

1. In a shallow dish or bowl, whisk together the eggs, milk, vanilla extract, and ground cinnamon until well combined.
2. Heat a cast iron skillet over medium heat and add the butter, allowing it to melt and coat the bottom of the skillet.
3. Dip each slice of bread into the egg mixture, turning to coat both sides evenly. Allow any excess egg mixture to drip off.
4. Place the dipped bread slices into the hot skillet, cooking 2 slices at a time if your skillet is not large enough to fit all 4 slices without crowding.
5. Cook the French toast for 2-3 minutes on each side, or until golden brown and crispy on the outside and cooked through on the inside.
6. Repeat with the remaining bread slices, adding more butter to the skillet if needed.
7. Serve the French toast hot, with maple syrup, powdered sugar, fresh berries, or sliced fruit on top if desired.

Enjoy your delicious cast iron skillet French toast for a cozy and satisfying breakfast or brunch!

Skillet Vegetable Paella

Ingredients:

- 1 tablespoon olive oil
- 1 onion, diced
- 2 cloves garlic, minced
- 1 bell pepper, diced
- 1 zucchini, diced
- 1 cup cherry tomatoes, halved
- 1 cup frozen peas
- 1 cup arborio rice
- 2 cups vegetable broth
- 1 teaspoon smoked paprika
- 1/2 teaspoon ground turmeric
- 1/2 teaspoon dried thyme
- Salt and pepper to taste
- Lemon wedges and chopped fresh parsley for garnish (optional)

Instructions:

1. Heat the olive oil in a large skillet over medium heat.
2. Add the diced onion to the skillet and cook until softened, about 5 minutes.
3. Stir in the minced garlic and cook for an additional 1-2 minutes, until fragrant.
4. Add the diced bell pepper, zucchini, cherry tomatoes, and frozen peas to the skillet. Cook for 5-7 minutes, or until the vegetables start to soften.
5. Stir in the arborio rice, smoked paprika, ground turmeric, and dried thyme, coating the rice and vegetables evenly with the spices.
6. Pour the vegetable broth into the skillet and stir to combine. Season with salt and pepper to taste.
7. Bring the mixture to a simmer, then reduce the heat to low. Cover the skillet with a lid and let the paella cook for 20-25 minutes, or until the rice is tender and the liquid has been absorbed. Stir occasionally to prevent sticking.
8. Once the rice is cooked, remove the skillet from the heat and let it sit, covered, for 5 minutes to allow the flavors to meld.
9. Fluff the paella with a fork and garnish with lemon wedges and chopped fresh parsley, if desired.
10. Serve the skillet vegetable paella hot, as a main dish or as a side dish with additional lemon wedges on the side.

Enjoy your delicious skillet vegetable paella, packed with colorful vegetables and aromatic spices for a tasty and satisfying meal!

Cast Iron Skillet Peach Pie

Ingredients:

For the Pie Crust:

- 2 1/2 cups all-purpose flour
- 1 teaspoon salt
- 1 tablespoon granulated sugar
- 1 cup unsalted butter, cold and cut into small cubes
- 6-8 tablespoons ice water

For the Peach Filling:

- 6-8 large ripe peaches, peeled, pitted, and sliced
- 1/2 cup granulated sugar (adjust according to the sweetness of the peaches)
- 1/4 cup brown sugar
- 2 tablespoons cornstarch
- 1 teaspoon ground cinnamon
- 1/4 teaspoon ground nutmeg
- 1 tablespoon lemon juice
- 1 teaspoon vanilla extract

For Assembly:

- 1 tablespoon unsalted butter, cut into small cubes
- 1 egg, beaten (for egg wash)
- 1 tablespoon granulated sugar (for sprinkling)

Instructions:

For the Pie Crust:

1. In a large mixing bowl, whisk together the flour, salt, and granulated sugar.
2. Add the cold cubed butter to the flour mixture. Using a pastry cutter or your fingers, cut the butter into the flour until the mixture resembles coarse crumbs.
3. Gradually add the ice water, 1 tablespoon at a time, mixing with a fork until the dough just comes together.
4. Divide the dough into two equal portions, shape each portion into a disk, wrap them in plastic wrap, and refrigerate for at least 30 minutes before using.

For the Peach Filling:

1. In a large bowl, combine the sliced peaches, granulated sugar, brown sugar, cornstarch, ground cinnamon, ground nutmeg, lemon juice, and vanilla extract. Toss until the

peaches are evenly coated with the sugar mixture. Let it sit for about 10-15 minutes to macerate.

For Assembly:

1. Preheat your oven to 375°F (190°C).
2. Roll out one disk of the chilled pie dough on a lightly floured surface into a circle large enough to fit the bottom and sides of your cast iron skillet. Transfer the dough to the skillet, gently pressing it into the bottom and up the sides.
3. Pour the macerated peach filling into the pie crust, spreading it out evenly.
4. Dot the top of the peach filling with small cubes of butter.
5. Roll out the second disk of chilled pie dough on a lightly floured surface into a circle large enough to cover the skillet. Carefully place it over the peach filling, sealing the edges with the bottom crust. Trim any excess dough and crimp the edges with a fork or your fingers to seal.
6. Cut slits in the top crust to allow steam to escape during baking.
7. Brush the top crust with the beaten egg and sprinkle with granulated sugar.
8. Place the skillet in the preheated oven and bake for 45-50 minutes, or until the crust is golden brown and the filling is bubbling.
9. Remove the skillet from the oven and let the pie cool for at least 30 minutes before serving.

Enjoy your delicious cast iron skillet peach pie, served warm with a scoop of vanilla ice cream or a dollop of whipped cream for a delightful dessert!

Skillet Chicken Marsala

Ingredients:

- 4 boneless, skinless chicken breasts
- Salt and pepper to taste
- 1/2 cup all-purpose flour
- 2 tablespoons olive oil
- 4 tablespoons unsalted butter, divided
- 8 ounces mushrooms, sliced
- 2 cloves garlic, minced
- 1 cup Marsala wine
- 1 cup chicken broth
- 1/2 cup heavy cream
- 2 tablespoons chopped fresh parsley (for garnish)
- Cooked pasta, rice, or mashed potatoes for serving (optional)

Instructions:

1. Place each chicken breast between two sheets of plastic wrap and gently pound them to an even thickness, about 1/2 inch thick. Season both sides of the chicken breasts with salt and pepper.
2. Place the flour in a shallow dish. Dredge each chicken breast in the flour, shaking off any excess.
3. In a large skillet, heat the olive oil and 2 tablespoons of butter over medium-high heat.
4. Add the chicken breasts to the skillet and cook for 4-5 minutes on each side, or until golden brown and cooked through. Remove the chicken from the skillet and set aside.
5. In the same skillet, add the remaining 2 tablespoons of butter. Once melted, add the sliced mushrooms and minced garlic. Cook, stirring occasionally, for about 5 minutes, or until the mushrooms are golden brown and tender.
6. Pour the Marsala wine into the skillet and bring to a simmer. Cook for 2-3 minutes, scraping up any browned bits from the bottom of the skillet.
7. Stir in the chicken broth and heavy cream. Bring the sauce to a simmer and cook for an additional 5-7 minutes, or until slightly thickened.
8. Return the cooked chicken breasts to the skillet, turning to coat them in the sauce. Let them simmer in the sauce for a few minutes to heat through.
9. Garnish the skillet chicken Marsala with chopped fresh parsley before serving.
10. Serve the chicken Marsala hot, with cooked pasta, rice, or mashed potatoes on the side if desired.

Enjoy your delicious skillet chicken Marsala, featuring tender chicken in a rich and flavorful Marsala wine sauce!

Cast Iron Skillet S'mores Dip

Ingredients:

- 1 cup semisweet chocolate chips
- 1 cup mini marshmallows
- 1 tablespoon unsalted butter
- Graham crackers, for dipping

Instructions:

1. Preheat your oven to 350°F (175°C).
2. Place the chocolate chips and unsalted butter in a cast iron skillet.
3. Transfer the skillet to the oven and bake for about 5-7 minutes, or until the chocolate chips are melted and smooth.
4. Carefully remove the skillet from the oven and sprinkle the mini marshmallows evenly over the melted chocolate.
5. Return the skillet to the oven and broil for 1-2 minutes, or until the marshmallows are golden brown and toasted. Keep a close eye on them to prevent burning.
6. Remove the skillet from the oven and let it cool for a few minutes before serving.
7. Serve the S'mores Dip hot, with graham crackers for dipping.

Enjoy your delicious cast iron skillet S'mores Dip, a gooey and irresistible dessert that's sure to be a hit at any gathering!

Skillet Sweet Potato Hash

Ingredients:

- 2 medium sweet potatoes, peeled and diced
- 1 bell pepper, diced
- 1 small onion, diced
- 2 cloves garlic, minced
- 2 tablespoons olive oil
- 1 teaspoon smoked paprika
- 1/2 teaspoon ground cumin
- Salt and pepper to taste
- Optional: chopped fresh parsley or green onions for garnish
- Optional: cooked bacon or sausage for added flavor

Instructions:

1. Heat the olive oil in a large skillet over medium heat.
2. Add the diced sweet potatoes to the skillet and cook for about 5-7 minutes, stirring occasionally, until they start to soften.
3. Add the diced bell pepper and onion to the skillet. Cook for an additional 5 minutes, or until the vegetables are tender and lightly caramelized.
4. Stir in the minced garlic, smoked paprika, ground cumin, salt, and pepper. Cook for another minute, until the garlic is fragrant and the spices are well combined with the vegetables.
5. If using cooked bacon or sausage, crumble it and add it to the skillet, stirring to combine with the vegetables.
6. Continue cooking the sweet potato hash for a few more minutes, until everything is heated through and the flavors have melded together.
7. Taste and adjust seasoning if necessary.
8. Garnish the skillet sweet potato hash with chopped fresh parsley or green onions before serving, if desired.

Enjoy your delicious skillet sweet potato hash as a satisfying and nutritious breakfast or brunch option! You can also serve it as a side dish with eggs or alongside your favorite protein for a complete meal.

Cast Iron Skillet Lemon Bars

Ingredients:

For the Crust:

- 1 cup all-purpose flour
- 1/4 cup granulated sugar
- 1/2 cup unsalted butter, cold and cubed

For the Lemon Filling:

- 4 large eggs
- 1 cup granulated sugar
- Zest of 2 lemons
- 1/2 cup fresh lemon juice (about 4-5 lemons)
- 2 tablespoons all-purpose flour
- 1/2 teaspoon baking powder
- Powdered sugar, for dusting

Instructions:

1. Preheat your oven to 350°F (175°C).
2. In a mixing bowl, combine the flour and granulated sugar for the crust. Add the cold cubed butter and use a pastry cutter or your fingers to mix until the mixture resembles coarse crumbs.
3. Press the crust mixture evenly into the bottom of a greased 10-inch cast iron skillet.
4. Bake the crust in the preheated oven for 15-20 minutes, or until lightly golden brown. Remove from the oven and set aside to cool slightly.
5. In another mixing bowl, whisk together the eggs, granulated sugar, lemon zest, lemon juice, flour, and baking powder until well combined.
6. Pour the lemon filling over the baked crust in the skillet.
7. Return the skillet to the oven and bake for an additional 20-25 minutes, or until the filling is set and the edges are lightly golden brown.
8. Remove the skillet from the oven and let the lemon bars cool completely in the skillet.
9. Once cooled, dust the top of the lemon bars with powdered sugar.
10. Slice the lemon bars into squares or wedges and serve.

Enjoy your delicious cast iron skillet lemon bars, with their tangy lemon filling and buttery crust, for a refreshing and delightful dessert!

Skillet Cajun Shrimp Pasta

Ingredients:

- 8 ounces linguine or fettuccine pasta
- 1 pound large shrimp, peeled and deveined
- 2 tablespoons Cajun seasoning
- Salt and pepper to taste
- 2 tablespoons olive oil
- 4 cloves garlic, minced
- 1 bell pepper, thinly sliced
- 1 small onion, thinly sliced
- 1 cup cherry tomatoes, halved
- 1 cup chicken broth
- 1 cup heavy cream
- 1/2 cup grated Parmesan cheese
- Fresh parsley, chopped, for garnish (optional)

Instructions:

1. Cook the pasta according to the package instructions until al dente. Drain and set aside.
2. In a mixing bowl, toss the shrimp with Cajun seasoning, salt, and pepper until evenly coated.
3. Heat olive oil in a large skillet over medium-high heat. Add the seasoned shrimp to the skillet and cook for 2-3 minutes on each side, or until pink and cooked through. Remove the shrimp from the skillet and set aside.
4. In the same skillet, add minced garlic, sliced bell pepper, and sliced onion. Cook for 2-3 minutes, or until the vegetables are softened.
5. Add halved cherry tomatoes to the skillet and cook for an additional 2-3 minutes, until they start to soften.
6. Pour chicken broth and heavy cream into the skillet. Bring the mixture to a simmer and cook for 2-3 minutes, stirring occasionally.
7. Stir in grated Parmesan cheese until melted and smooth, creating a creamy sauce.
8. Add the cooked pasta and cooked shrimp back to the skillet. Toss everything together until the pasta and shrimp are coated evenly with the sauce.
9. Cook for an additional 2-3 minutes, or until everything is heated through.
10. Remove the skillet from the heat and garnish with chopped fresh parsley, if desired.
11. Serve the Cajun shrimp pasta hot, with additional Parmesan cheese on the side if desired.

Enjoy your delicious skillet Cajun shrimp pasta, with its spicy Cajun flavor and creamy sauce, for a satisfying and flavorful meal!